WRITE YOUR OWN

Please return this book to the library on or before the last date stamped below.

To Poppy – a hobbit,
starting on her journey

First published in the UK in 2004 by Chrysalis Children's Books,
An imprint of Chrysalis Books Group,
The Chrysalis Building, Bramley Rd, London W10 6SP

Copyright © Chrysalis Books Group PLC 2004
Text copyright © Pie Corbett 2004

Editorial Manager: Joyce Bentley
Editor: Debbie Foy
Designer: Sophie Wilkins
Illustrator: Peter Bailey

ISBN 1 84458 324 4

British Library Cataloguing in Publication Data for
this book is available from the British Library.

Printed and bound in China

10 9 8 7 6 5 4 3 2 1

CONTENTS

FLIGHTS OF FANTASY
THINKING ABOUT FANTASY

Silva stared at the stones that lay on either side of the path. She was sure that she had seen one move. She peered closer and one of the stones winked at her with a bright, golden eye. She picked it up. It was as cold and hard as a stone should be, so she gave it a squeeze. It let out a sudden and terrible shriek!

At that moment all the other stones seemed to wake. They shouted at Silva, whistling and yelling in a chorus of gravelly voices. Then the boulder spoke.

'Put my cousin down,' it said in a low, gruff voice. Its eyes flickered dangerously. You could hardly see the thin line of its mouth or its grey, sharp teeth.

If you like the sort of story where the impossible can occur, then you like fantasy! Fantasy is great to write because you can really let your imagination run riot – stones can chatter, people can become invisible and orcs can lurk in the subway!

Try your hand at a fantasy story. As the writer, it's up to you....

WHAT IS FANTASY?

Fantasy stories always contain an element of impossibility – new worlds, weird creatures, and a good dose of magical happenings.

A fantasy story can be:

☆ **'Myths and legends'** fantasy
Trolls, giant sea serpents, elves, goblins, fairies, pixies, or a golden phoenix may feature in these stories.

☆ **'New-universe'** fantasy
In these stories different worlds are created, as in the *Narnia* stories where the children enter a new world through the back of a wardrobe. In this type of fantasy story, characters will often reach the new universe through a magical portal or gateway, for example:

☆ a bewitched mirror;
☆ a painting that comes alive;
☆ a dark attic;
☆ a whispering tunnel.

When writing 'new-universe' fantasy make sure that the new world that you invent is believable enough for the reader to relate to!

☆ **'Change'** fantasy

In these stories the main characters change dramatically but remain within our world. For example, miniature people who live under the floorboards or teachers that can fly!

☆ **'History'** fantasy

These stories usually involve:

☆ altering our history, for example: life in medieval times was ruled by intelligent rats;

☆ predicting the future, for example: by 2099 schools will be run by robots;

☆ life after a catastrophic event, for example: a massive meteorite explosion or a devastating space war.

☆ **'Magic'** fantasy

These involve characters, such as Harry Potter, using magic. 'Fantasy schools', featuring apprentice wizards who are learning magic with disastrous results, is a popular and fun story type.

☆ **'Fighting'** fantasy

Fighting fantasies give the reader a choice at the end of each scene so that you can find different 'routes' through the story.

WRITING TIP

Some of the writing terms in this book are explained in the glossary on page 62.

WHAT DO I NEED TO WRITE MY OWN FANTASY?

The good thing about writing is that you don't need much equipment, just a notebook, a pen and a place to write. You can write almost anywhere: a park bench, on top of a bus, or lying on your bed. Some writers prefer to write directly onto the computer.  You will need a good dictionary to check spellings (or a computer spell-check) and a thesaurus to help find alternatives to words you use a lot.

CAPTIVATING READING!

If you want to be a good fantasy writer then you have to read plenty. When you are reading, note how writers make events sound 'out of this world', freakish or captivating!

This is a list of my favourite fantasy books. Try to read as many as possible to really get a feel for fantasy writing.

- ☆ *The Chronicles of Narnia*, CS Lewis
- ☆ *Wolf Tower* series, Tanith Lee
- ☆ *Chrestomanci* series, Dianne Wynne Jones
- ☆ *Snow Spider Trilogy*, Jenny Nimmo
- ☆ *The Snow Walker's Son*, Catherine Fisher
- ☆ *The Sterkarm Handshake*, Susan Price
- ☆ *Harry Potter* series, JK Rowling

☆ *The Switchers* series, Kate Thompson
☆ *The Hobbit*, JR Tolkein
☆ *The Key to the Lost Kingdom*, Jay Ashton
☆ *The Dark is Rising* series, Susan Cooper
☆ *Krindlekrax*, Philip Ridley
☆ *The BFG*, Roald Dahl
☆ *Northern Lights* trilogy, Philip Pullman
☆ *The Edge Chronicles*, Paul Stewart and Chris Riddell
☆ *Eragon*, Christopher Paolini

WRITING TIP

To become a good writer of fantastical tales you must read as many as possible. Visit your local library or school library and take out fantasy novels. Always have a book by your bed and make it a habit to read every night. Read, read and then read some more!

KEEP A WRITING JOURNAL

When you dream up a fantastic idea write it down, otherwise you may forget it! Most writers keep a writing journal in which they jot down ideas that come to them, perhaps sparked off by something they have seen or heard. Make your own journal out of a jotter or exercise book – a blank notebook with a hard cover is ideal. Carry it with you everywhere and get into the habit of making notes while walking to school, waiting for a bus, or even at the swimming pool!

Look out for:

☆ Strange-looking people who might be visitors from another planet;

☆ Unusual places that could be a portal to another world;

☆ Weird objects that could possess special powers;

☆ Peculiar events that could only be explained by magic.

OUTLANDISH IDEAS

Writers are always on the lookout for ideas. Like curious elves, they keep their eyes and ears open for ideas they might gather for their story. A great way to start thinking about fantasy stories is to make a list of ideas using 'What if...' or 'Supposing...'

What if...

☆ you could see the future in a mirror;

☆ your bicycle could fly;

☆ you met a dog that could talk;

☆ you were given an invisibility cloak;

☆ you stepped in a puddle and sank into another world.

Supposing...

☆ whatever you touched turned into gold;

☆ you could read people's thoughts;

☆ you found a goblin hiding in your sock drawer;

☆ you travel to another world and cannot return until you find a precious object.

TIME TO WRITE

1 Start off your writing journal with a list of your favourite authors and thrillers. Jot down why you like these authors and books.

2 Now start collecting some ideas. Jot down:
★ Freakish or unusual happenings;
★ Weird–looking people from other lands;
★ Bizarre places;
★ Strange or enchanted objects.

3 Make a list of 'What if...' or 'Supposing...' ideas in your writing journal. Try putting odd things together, for example, a snake that talks or a mountain that glows in the dark.

4 Take your best idea and start daydreaming about what might happen in the story. Keep coming back to the story idea and see how much of it you can daydream. Make notes in your journal so you don't forget what happens. Later on you can use the daydream (or parts of it) as a basis for a story.

WRITERS AT WORK

STARTING YOUR OWN STORY

Many fantasy stories are based on a journey or 'quest' in which the main character has to travel in order to fulfill a task. All writers have five 'servants' to help them when they sit down to write: who? where? when? what? and how?

1. Who?

You need a main character –
a good, strong heroine or hero.
This person may come from
humble origins and be the third
daughter of a goatkeeper! At
the start of the story, your main
character might feel afraid and

may find the whole idea of an adventure very bothersome! Don't worry – as the story unfolds the main character will learn new skills and prove to be resourceful, loyal and brave. This character may also have companions. These could be: a dwarf, a prince or princess, a hobbit, an elf, or even a wizard.

In fantasy stories there is usually a character who is the 'helper'. This character may appear at difficult moments and save the main character from foolishness or disaster.

Your 'helper' could be
☆ a magical creature, like a
   leprechaun;
☆ a unicorn;
☆ a golden eagle;
☆ an owl;
☆ a wizard;
☆ a clever raven.

In some stories the main character is helped by visiting a magical place, for example: a lake that is enchanted, a magical waterfall, a cave that tells fortunes, or a tree that gives advice to travellers! Your characters could also be helped by a magical object such as a ring, a cloak, or a box of wishes.

WRITING TIP

Jot down ideas for your main character. Make a list of companions for the journey – don't have too many or it will get confusing! Then divide a page of your journal into four columns and make lists of possible 'helpers' under the headings: 'human helpers', 'magical creatures', 'enchanted places' and 'magical objects.'

---

2. Where?

You will need to decide where to set your story and where your characters are going on their quest.

They might have to travel:
☆ across treacherous mountain ranges;
☆ through damp, underground tunnels and mines;
☆ through bewitched, dark forests;
☆ across endless, dry deserts;
☆ through eerie, deserted
   cities on distant planets.

It may help to draw a 'story map' showing the journey your characters will take. Draw onto the map the different places that they visit.

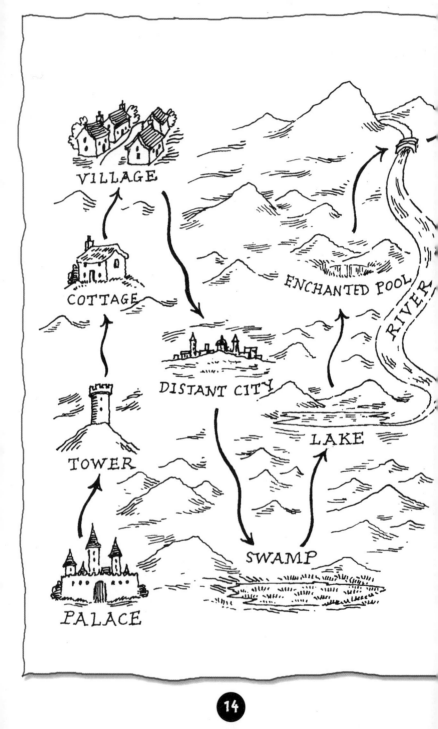

VILLAGE

COTTAGE

ENCHANTED POOL

RIVER

DISTANT CITY

TOWER

LAKE

PALACE

SWAMP

DESERT

SEA

ENTRANCE TO
UNDERGROUND MINES

FOREST

ICY TERRAIN

VOLCANO

MOUNTAIN
RANGE

FOSSILISED TREE

CAVES

EAGLE'S NEST

3. When?

Most stories are set in the past. This makes it sound as though the action has already happened, for example: *Zane took a deep breath and rubbed the magic ring.*

Writing in the present tense can be exciting as it sounds as if the action is happening now: *Zane takes a deep breath and rubs the magic ring.* Whether you decide to write in the past or present tense, remember to stick with it. If you slip from one tense to another you may confuse your readers!

You may also want to consider when the journey will start. What will the weather be like? This plays an important part in setting the scene and creating the right atmosphere. For example, the weather is likely to be dark and gloomy as the travellers set off on a difficult journey.

4. What?

You need to decide what the task is and what your main character has to do on this journey. Is the task to find something or someone?

☆ a magic potion for the dying king?

☆ an enchanted key to open a buried box?

☆ a captured elf king?

Or perhaps the task is to take something
or someone to a particular place:
- ☆ the last unicorn to its rightful land?
- ☆ a magical ring to its owner?
- ☆ a wicked goblin to the gates of
  the underworld?
- ☆ a long-lost princess back to her
  kingdom?

WRITING TIP

Make a list of ideas for different tasks. Ask
other people for ideas and think about the ideas
you have read in books, seen on television or in films.
Put a star by your best ideas.

You will also need to decide what sort of obstacles your
characters will encounter. In your story, each obstacle
could take up a paragraph or two.

The obstacles could be:
- ☆ extraordinary creatures such
  as man-eating goblins, giant
  spiders, savage vines;
- ☆ natural forces such as storms,
  starbursts, deserts or shipwrecks;
- ☆ getting trapped, entangled,
  poisoned or chased;
- ☆ having to solve problems such
  as codes, riddles or mazes.

5. How?

You will need to decide how your main characters

overcome the obstacles put in their way. Perhaps they have a bewitched or magical object such as a sword, ring, lucky rabbit's foot or toad? Or maybe they use special powers like hypnotism, laser-vision, invisibility or casting spells. But perhaps it will be sheer cunning that saves the day! Sometimes the main character will be saved by someone who is repaying them for a previous act of kindness. That's why it pays for adventurers to share their food with any beggars they meet and to rescue animals that might be hurt or trapped!

WRITING TIP

Draw onto your story map sketches of the obstacles, disasters or evil creatures that await your characters as they journey on their task.

THE MAGICAL RULE

You may have noticed that in many fantasies things happens in threes. To writers, this is known as the magical 'rule of three'. For example, have your characters encounter three main obstacles in

their journey. To make the ending really captivating, save the most exciting part of the story until the end. Let the main characters fail twice in the final task but succeed on the third occasion. This helps to build up the tension and keeps your reader mesmerised!

THE HOMECOMING

Fantasy stories are commonly rounded off with a splendid homecoming party in honour of the weary travellers. Often the main characters have learned something or have changed for the better as a result of their quest. For example: a selfish princess learns to be generous; a bad-tempered wizard resolves to be kinder; a crafty gnome stops looking for mischief.

1 In your writing journal make some notes about:

Who? Jot down ideas for your main characters, companions and helpers.

Where? Write down some ideas for where they will travel on the quest. It helps to draw a story map and put in all the places to be visited.

When? Will you write your story in the past or the present? Write a few sample sentences and see which seems more effective.

What? Decide on the task that your main character has to carry out.

How? Make a list to show how your characters will defeat the perils they come across on their journey.

2 Draw a story map. Make it clear where the story starts and where your characters are going.

Draw onto the map the obstacles that will have to be overcome. Make notes about how they will overcome these obstacles.

TRICKS OF THE TRADE
How to captivate your readers!

All the best writers do a lot of thinking before putting pen to paper. Once you have some ideas about the plot outline, you need to think about how to create characters and settings that will really grip your readers.

MAKING YOUR CHARACTERS 'REAL'

Usually the main character is quite ordinary. Often he or she doesn't really want to go on the quest, preferring to stay at home where it is safe and comfortable.
Your main character may be rather shy and scared of adventure. In this way, you can show character development as, by the end of the story, a new and stronger person will have emerged!

1. Name your characters
Give your characters fantastical names that will add to the atmosphere of your story. For example, Delores Witchmass, Zeb Noggin, Zane Vinesnap or Stargazer!

2. Describe your characters

To make your characters 'jump off the page', you will need to describe their appearance. Don't give too much detail, as sometimes it is better to leave just a little bit to the reader's imagination!

☆ **What their clothes are like**

For example, *the dwarf wore a red cloak the colour of holly berries* or *her black velvet gown swayed as she walked.*

☆ **How they act**

For example, *the old man dashed about behind the counter, fetching the ingredients, muttering to himself* or *she looked furtively around like a rabbit sneaking out of its hole.*

☆ **How they look**

For example, *her hands were like claws* or *its eyes were like fierce, black buttons and its mouth was small and mean.*

☆ **What they carry with them**

In his hand he held a bright, crystal eye or *a pig trotted along behind the witch and Zennor could have sworn that it was about to speak.*

3. How your characters feel

How does your main character feel at the start of the journey? They might be: sad, lonely, angry, unhappy, afraid, nervous, mean, spiteful, excited, bossy?

Make a few notes in your writing journal about *why* they might be feeling like this. Sometimes the main character starts the story with a negative feeling – maybe she is rather spoilt and can be selfish. By the end of the story she may have changed for the better – and no longer acts in a spoilt, selfish manner.

☆ Make your characters reluctant

It can help to add depth to the main character if the author shows them wishing for home, regretting they had ever become involved:

Zennor picked up her ice pick. She felt a sudden pang of loss. How she wished she was back in the homestead, sitting in front of her little stove with the kettle singing and the smell of jam bubbling in the cooking pot....

This can be followed by the main character resolving to continue with

the quest, whatever problems they might encounter on the way: *But she brushed back her tears and stared into the distance.*
Somewhere out there the Elf Prince waited. And Zennor was the only person who could save him.
She gritted her teeth and continued to climb the craggy mountain...

☆ **Make your characters have a special fear!**

Early in the story, plant the idea in your reader's mind that the main character does not like something, for example: dragons, orcs, witches, darkness, snakes, or marsh people. If you do this, the reader knows for sure that the object of fear is bound to pop up on the journey! Read this example:

Zennor had never liked spiders. She drove her mother crazy by screaming at the tiny, red spiders that lived on the barn roof. The thought of giant spiders was something that she didn't even wish to consider. She shuddered, squeezed her eyes tight and followed Zeb into the cave...

4. Making your characters talk

Show what your characters are like and how they are feeling through what they say and how they say it. Use adverbs to tell your readers how a character speaks. An ancient goblin might speak slowly and carefully while a young elf might speak quickly and breathlessly. Other fantasy characters may speak savagely, fearlessly, cautiously, bravely and so on. You might also want to use a speech verb every now and then. For example: he mumbled, whispered, groaned, hissed, bellowed, roared…

Different characters would say different things. For example, imagine a situation in which a character meets a cruel goblin who is behaving badly. Let's put a brave character and a shy character into the same situation and see how they speak and behave in different ways:

☆ **Brave character**

The goblin poked the donkey again and even though it was laden with sacks of gold, it hobbled forwards. Zennor rushed up the path, jumping over the stream until she had caught up. 'Stop that,' she yelled, grabbing the goblin by the shoulder and spinning him round….

☆ **Shy character**

The goblin poked the donkey again and even though it was laden with sacks of gold, it hobbled

forwards. Zinnia paused at the stream and took several seconds to pluck up the courage to jump across.
'Excuse me,' she whispered. But the dwarf ignored her and, giving the donkey another sharp prod, carried on up the path....

Have you ever read a story where the dialogue goes crazy? For example:

'Hi.'
'Hi.'
'Watch out.'
'OK.'
'Oh no!'
'Thank goodness!'

Too much speech becomes confusing and the reader forgets who is speaking. You can avoid this problem by limiting the exchanges of speech.

To help your reader picture what is happening as a character speaks, add a supporting action. For example:
'I have no intention of journeying anywhere,' muttered Genie, as she dropped another sugar beetle into the rat's mouth.
The word 'as' allows you to add what the character is doing and breaks the dialogue up.

CREATING COMPANIONS

Companions to the main character are an important part of fantasy writing. When thinking about companions it can help to make a sketch and write some descriptive notes in your journal. You could choose one of these as a companion:

A dwarf

☆ short with a long beard;
☆ expert at mining gold;
☆ a famous sword-maker;
☆ grumbles when on journeys as he prefers being underground;
☆ sings songs about past dwarfish deeds;
☆ extremely loyal.

An elf

☆ small, slim and beautiful;
☆ young-looking but ancient in years;
☆ performs magic and can often fly;
☆ can lure folk with magical singing;
☆ enjoys woods, mountains and lakes.

A princess

☆ beautiful and fiery-tempered;

☆ able to disguise herself well;

☆ good at archery, riding and saving the day;

☆ at first keeps her identity hidden;

☆ may be seeking her brother, kidnapped by a wicked goblin at birth;

☆ carries a secret flask of enchanted water that can save lives.

A prince

☆ eager to please, but sometimes clumsy;

☆ may lead you into trouble by mistake;

☆ brave and fiercely loyal;

☆ good at riding and sword fighting;

☆ may be unaware he is a prince and rightful heir to throne;

☆ perhaps has a lost identical twin.

DREAMS, DESIRES, FORTUNES AND WISHES

To create really spellbinding, outlandish characters you need to give them a special talent, motivation or power they might use for good or bad!

Perhaps your character:

☆ has a secret that no-one else knows;

☆ has a dream or wish that comes true;

☆ tells a lie and things go badly as a result;

☆ can predict the future;

☆ can morph into objects or creatures.

NAME: FARSIGHT

AGE: 120 YEARS

ADDRESS: EAGLE'S MOUNT, THE GREAT WASTE

DESCRIPTION: A WARRIOR WITH WINGS LIKE AN EAGLE

SPECIAL ABILITIES: FLIES AND CAN SEE FOR MILES

WEAPONS: BOW AND ARROWS

LIKES: BEING ALONE

DISLIKES: CROWDS OR ANY CLOSED-IN SPACE SUCH AS CAVES. WOULD HATE BEING TRAPPED IN A PRISON

REASON FOR TRAVELLING: TO FIND THE LOST TRIBE OF EAGLE WARRIORS

VISIONARY CREATURES

In a fantasy quest you are bound to meet a whole host of fantastical creatures. For example:

☆ a city dragon;
☆ a hunchback ferryman;
☆ a talking eagle;
☆ a mischievous hedge-pixie;
☆ a wounded unicorn;
☆ a terrifying troll.

Your readers will already know what some of these creatures look like through reading books or watching films, so you may only need a little description to bring them alive. Try selecting one or two details and drop them into the story: *The dwarf sat down. Zeb stared at his pointy, scarlet slippers. They were too big and made the dwarf look ridiculous...*

Of course, you may want to invent a totally new creature. This is easy enough if you take something you already know and change it in one or two ways. For example, you could have:

☆ a ferocious rabbit;
☆ a miniature elephant;
☆ a talking eagle;
☆ a mouse with long, spindly legs;
☆ a gigantic, yellow beetle.

WRITING TIP

Use 'sentences of three' to build up a description of your characters. For example:

'The dwarf was shorter than a child, dressed in a long red cloak and carried an axe.'

'The Queen wore a shimmering dress of silver, carried a thin sword and wore shoes that ended in sharp daggers.'

'The troll had an ugly face, massive hairy warts and hands like spades.'

SPELLBINDING SETTINGS

Your journey could lead anywhere. For example, you may travel:

☆ through an ocean Kingdom;
☆ to a submerged island;
☆ through a dark forest;
☆ across a desert;
☆ to a ruined city;
☆ over an enchanted bridge;
☆ into a lush, green valley.

1. Use place names

Use the story map to locate different places your travellers will pass through. Invent unusual place names to bring the settings alive. For example, if your companions are about to step into 'Hangman's Forest' then we only need to suggest that it is dark and the trees are close together to build up the picture of a threatening place.

2. Use weather and time of day

Weather and time of day are important in creating atmosphere in your story. If your travellers are passing

across a mountain ridge on a hot, sunny afternoon then little will happen. But if a storm starts brewing then we imagine that disaster will soon strike.

3. Create the 'impossible'

Fantasy settings may seem challenging at first but the secret is to use what you know and then add a few surprising or 'impossible' elements.

For instance, supposing we wanted to create a palace set in another world. Use a few 'real' details and then add in some 'impossible' things:

☆ **Creatures**, for example: miniature elephants that serve at the table or a sharp-eyed hawk that acts as nanny to the children;

☆ **Objects**, for example: a mirror that tells you the truth or a chandelier that doubles as a gigantic playswing;

☆ **Features**, for example: a fire that can burn cold or hot, depending on how you feel or a bottomless pool;

☆ **Plants**, for example: a barking beanstalk that acts as a 'guard dog' or a creeping vine that can 'write' messages.

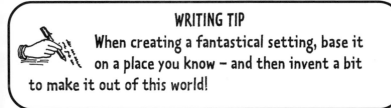
4. Throw in some surprises!

Catch your reader off guard by taking something in the setting and bringing it alive! This will grab their attention and make them want to find out more!

For example:

☆ Tim gazed up at both the silvery moons...

☆ The rock winked at her...

☆ At that moment the tree bowed and spoke...

☆ The blankets wrapped themselves around her and the pillow sang a lullaby...

STYLISH SENTENCES

Writers choose their words carefully, sometimes rewriting one sentence many times to make it sound right! Here are some ideas for adding a professional touch to your story:

1. Just for starters

What do you think of this paragraph? *Jaff went down the road. He popped into the broomstick shop. He bought a broomstick. He came outside. He sat on it. He took off for home.*

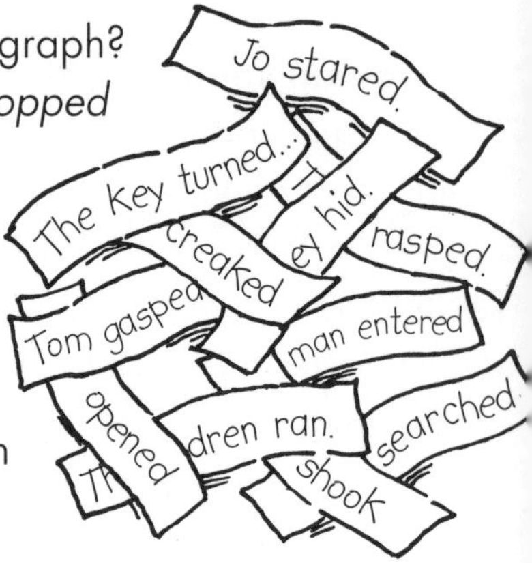

Yes, the writing sounds dull because all the sentences begin in the same way.

Jo stared.
The key turned...
creaked
ey hid.
rasped
Tom gasped
man entered
opened
dren ran.
searched
Th
shook

Try to vary the start of your sentences to keep your reader's attention. Here are some suggestions:

☆ Start with a connective:
Although he was tall for an elf, Giblin could just squeeze through the giant's keyhole.

☆ Start with an adverb:
Quickly, he handed the giantess the enchanted harp.

☆ Start with an 'ing' word:
Grabbing the chalice, he drank swiftly.

☆ Start with a simile:
Like an ogre, the tunnel roared.
As quick as an eel, he spun round.

As the key turned as while Tom stared in the the door the key rasped. Although packed. It opened so that man enter could hide. As the ro of search hey shook.

34

2. Spice it up!

What do you think of this paragraph?
Something howled in the cave. Zeb listened. Zink cried. A shadow fell over them. A wolfman peered down. His teeth gleamed. His claws flexed. The children fled. They hid. They shivered. The wolfman pursued them.
Yes, too many short sentences sound odd.

Is this paragraph better?
Something howled in the cave while the wind blew. Zeb listened and Zink cried. A shadow fell over them as a

wolfman peered down. His teeth gleamed and his claws flexed. The children fled and they hid. They shivered as the wolfman pursued them. This time the writing sounds odd because there are too many compound sentences.

Finally, read this:
Zeb listened. Something howled in the cave. What could it be? Zink gasped! A shadow fell over them as a wolfman

peered down. His teeth gleamed and his claws flexed. Without thinking, the children fled and hid behind the singing rock. They shivered as the creature pursued them… This time the writing is better because different types of sentences are used.

☆ Questions draw your reader into the story: *But what could it be?*

35

☆ Exclamations are good for dramatic moments:
Zink gasped!

☆ Short sentences create tension: *Zeb listened.*

☆ Simple sentences keep things clear: *Something howled in the cave.*

☆ Compound sentences are easy to read and keep the story flowing: *His teeth gleamed and his claws flexed.*

☆ Complex sentences add extra information: *Without a further thought, the children fled and hid behind the singing rock.*

TIME TO WRITE

You are almost ready to start your story. First, brainstorm some ideas and jot them down in your writing journal. Think about:

★ Character's names and descriptions including one distinctive detail. What are they wearing and what are they carrying with them?

★ Any special talents or powers?

★ How they feel about the adventure.

★ Is the main character reluctant (and why)?

★ What are they most afraid of?

★ Draw and make notes about any unusual creatures they will meet.

★ List key places on the quest and name them.

★ Practise different sentence types and save any good ideas for your story.

★ Spend time day-dreaming about your characters and what might happen to them.

PUTTING PEN TO PAPER

KICK-START YOUR WRITING

Ready to start writing? Before you finally start, read this chapter. Each section will help you through a different stage in your fantasy quest.

MAKING A FLYING START

Imagine if you read a fantasy story that started like this: *Jake woke up, went down for breakfast, ate his cornflakes and went to school.* Doesn't exactly grip you, does it? The start of your story must really captivate your reader and make them itch to find out more! Here are some ideas.

1. Start with the name of your main character

For example, *Zeb peered down the jet black hole, took a deep breath, and plunged in.* This kind of opening not only introduces the main character straight away, it also helps to get the action going.

2. Use an exclamation or command

For example: *'Flying while on guard is forbidden!'
snapped the gaoler.* This provides a surprise at the start
of the story that will grab your reader's interest.

3. Use weather or time of day

For example: *It was dark and forbidding in
Crowfast, with grey clouds scudding
across the sky...*

4. Use a fantasy setting

For example: *The bewitched
towers were made of glass.
Zennor could see the great
staircases, stretching upwards...*

5. Use a dramatic event

For example: *Farsight woke
at once. Something was in his
room, slithering across the floor
towards him.* This plunges your
reader straight into the story.

6. Use a fantasy object

*In the hallway the carpets
were busy dusting themselves
down and the chairs scuttled
back into position by the
great table...*

BEST FOOT FORWARD – THE TASK!

1. Introduce the task

Early on you need to introduce the task that sets the characters off on their quest. They might be looking for:

✩ A sacred cup, stolen by an eagle warrior that is now needed to restore peace;

✩ An invisibility ring needed to sneak into enemy territory;

✩ A stone that holds the power of good to save the land;

✩ A magical potion to save the dying queen.

2. Starting off on the quest

Early in the story the main character usually meets companions. Together they set off to fulfill the quest. You will also need to introduce the 'helper' who may not stay for the whole journey but who might appear every so often to help with sticky situations.

The helper often warns the travellers not to do, say, use or touch something but the travellers will usually ignore this advice and get into some sort of danger, as a result.

'You must stay this side of the mountain,' said Crest, as the dwarves peered over his

shoulder at the great map.

'But it'll be quicker to go the other way,' muttered Silva.
Crest turned to face her.

'I tell you – do not leave the path and wander to the other side. That way lies danger!' Crest pointed at the map and on the far side of the mountain a stain of blood began to grow and spread…

WRITING TIP

In the first or second paragraph introduce the quest and set the travellers off on their journey. Provide warnings and hints about the dangers that lurk ahead.

ADDING SHAPE TO YOUR STORY

Think of a fantasy quest story as a series of scenes. Each scene is built around the travellers reaching another place on the story map. Here there is another challenge to overcome. A good idea is to write a brief outline of your scenes on mini sticky labels and stick them onto the map.

Try using the 'rule of three' for each scene. In the following story outline there are three escape attempts, and success is achieved on the third attempt. The 'rule of three' is useful here because if your characters get over difficulties too easily, then your story runs the risk of being dull. Keep your readers on the edge of their seats! To do this is quite simple. Your scenes could take this shape:

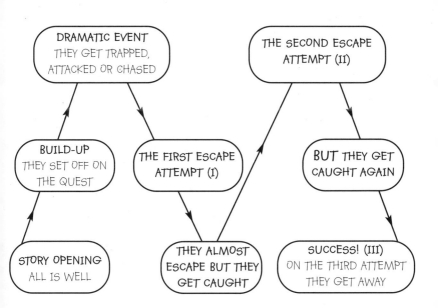

DRAMATIC EVENT
THEY GET TRAPPED, ATTACKED OR CHASED

THE SECOND ESCAPE ATTEMPT (II)

BUILD-UP
THEY SET OFF ON THE QUEST

THE FIRST ESCAPE ATTEMPT (I)

BUT THEY GET CAUGHT AGAIN

STORY OPENING
ALL IS WELL

THEY ALMOST ESCAPE BUT THEY GET CAUGHT

SUCCESS! (III)
ON THE THIRD ATTEMPT THEY GET AWAY

ZAP! POW! – WRITING ACTION SCENES

Action scenes are a vital part of a fantasy quest as your characters will have many challenges to face and will need to get out of many scrapes. Here are some ideas for writing gripping action scenes:

1. Use a 'sentence of three' to build up pace:
Zennor leaped over the hedge, seized the goblin and shook it like a rat.

2. Use powerful verbs to:

☆ add 'punch' to your writing.
Compare these two sentences
and you'll see what I mean:
*Shardi <u>went</u> forwards, <u>got hold</u> of
the ladder and <u>went</u> up into the trees.*
*Shardi <u>dashed</u> forwards, <u>gripped</u> the ladder and
<u>hoisted</u> himself up into the trees.*

☆ describe action:
Grab, grip, grasp, seize, squeeze, squash, punch,
hit, dig, poke, prod, leap, jump, vault, rush, dash,
swing, run....

☆ describe noise:
Crunch, squeal, scream, spit, hiss, whisper, shout, yell,
moan, groan, howl....

ACTION STATIONS: THE FANTASY SCENES
Most fantasy quest stories involve the main characters
making a journey in difficult and dangerous
circumstances. Here are four
captivating places that travellers
may encounter on their quest:

1. The Remarkable River Crossing
In fantasy stories a river crossing is
very common. It may be miles to
the nearest bridge and so the
travellers have to plunge into the

icy river. Inevitably, they will lose their footing and one or more will be swept away. Usually they will be rescued or appear later on in the story. Provisions, like food, may be lost, as will an object of value that the travellers rely on.

In many fantasies the travellers have to cross the river to escape something or someone. Many evil creatures will not enter water and so the river crossing is a method of escape or a barrier. A character with special powers, such as a wizard, may be able to make the river swallow attackers.

If there is a bridge, be careful. These may crumble half way across and almost certainly there will be something evil lurking in the water or guarding the way.

At the bridge, Silva paused. She could hear the orcs behind her, screaming as they poured through the forest. She only had a few seconds to act. She took out the tiny box that Crest had given her. His final words echoed in her ears: 'Do not flinch from danger – the oracle will protect you.' She opened the silver box and whispered, 'Help us across, keep back the orcs.'

Boatmen may offer a ride on a small punt across the river. But beware! They have often been chained by magic to ferry people across the river for eternity. Though gruff and bad-tempered, their eyes will gleam at the sight of gold as they have a tendency to be greedy. On no account should any of your characters take the boatman's oars if offered

them, as this may be part of a charm that releases the boatman from the spell, but binds your companion to it forever!

When rowing across a river a mist may appear. This is usually just before a creature –

perhaps a sea serpent – attacks the boat. Serpents often coil themselves around the boat and attempt to crush it. You may be lucky and come across a small village harbour. Here there will be river elves. They are nearly always friendly and will help out if you are in trouble.

2. The Far-Fetched Forest

In a fantasy quest your travellers will usually have to pass through a forest. Forests are often deceptive. They may be sunny at first, with open spaces and sheltered 'glades', but as the journey continues the trees may close together and tower high above the travellers. It is usually dark and difficult to stay on the path. Sometimes there are no paths at all and travellers may get lost. Forests are seen as a waste of the travellers' precious time as important tasks cannot be fulfilled.

The trees have a nasty habit of coming alive. They are often threatening and are prone to trap poor travellers in a 'prison' of branches. Their roots can also wrap like tentacles around the bodies of unsuspecting sleepers.

Gardri settled back against a tree, closed his eyes and began to sleep. And as he dreamed of dwarfish pleasures, of distant mountains, defeating dragons and finding treasure, the others too, curled up to sleep.

Silently, a thin stem of what looked like ivy, snaked out from the tree and began to coil itself about Gardri's legs. A moment later he was bound fast...

Many nasty things lurk in the forest. There may be giant spiders whose webs are so sticky that once you are stuck only a magic sword can slice through the threads and release you. The spiders will be enormous, have huge eyes and eat human flesh. Spiders will not bargain with you or take up a

45

challenge to fight, preferring instead to spin a steel-like cocoon around intruders.

On entering a forest most travellers almost always sense that they are being watched. Often a warning shot is fired and a spear or arrow whizzes past. If there are forest-dwellers they may use nets to capture travellers or have ropes or ladders that suddenly drop down. They will live in tree houses in 'forest cities' hidden far above the ground in the treetops. This may involve runways and bridges made of vines woven together.

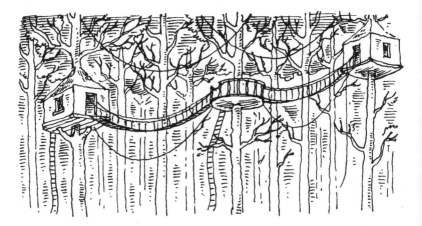

Elves also live in forests. They are small, slim and usually beautiful. They live to a great age but always look young. They are renowned for their music-making and are skilled with a bow. Often they can be persuaded to assist travellers so have to be treated with great respect. An encounter with Elves will be scary but also thrilling, as there are so few left. Many have died away as humans are destroying their natural world.

WRITING TIP

 Try using these special devices to make your writing more powerful:

1. Alliteration
This is the repetition of similar sounds. It can add atmosphere to your writing. In this example the 's' sound is repeated: The sly snake slipped into the magician's pocket...

2. Onomatopoeia
Words that sound like their meaning. In the snake hissed and spat, the repetition of the 's' sound helps to create the hissing sound of the snake.

3. Similes
A simile is a way of comparing one thing with another. Either use the word 'like': The unicorn's saddle looked like a flat mushroom. Or use the word 'as': His gold ring was as thin as a strand of giant's hair.

4. Metaphors
Metaphors are when one thing becomes another – they are a form of magic themselves! They help create captivating pictures: The red-faced sun peered down at the travellers.

5. Personification
Personification makes an object seem human. You might describe an object as though it looks human: The gnarled, old tree held out its arms. Or describe it as if it is doing something a human might do: The trees moaned in the wind. Personification is a form of powerful magic that writers use to bring their world alive!

3. The Deserted City Scene

Any fantasy quest will involve travelling to a city. There are many different types of city. Often there is a high wall and entry is by one gate. This will be guarded, so an ingenious method is needed to enter. This could involve disguise or hiding in a cart. Gatemen are often surly and will not believe an honest traveller so have to be deceived. Gatemen may also be prone to getting drunk. Luckily, this may provide an opportunity for entry as they will often fall asleep while on duty. Secret tunnels or long-hidden side gates may be useful.

Silva stood outside the city gates and waited. For a long

time nothing happened. Then a small, wooden shutter opened and a red-faced, drunken man spoke. 'Whaddaya want?' he slurred. Silva smiled at him and held out a few silver coins. The shutter slammed and she could hear somebody fumbling with keys. The side gate opened and the gatekeeper came out. He was enormously fat, his belly poking out over his belt. He peered at the coins and Silva could smell the alcohol on his breath...

Inside the city there will be beggars, traders, and many dark alleyways to avoid. Alleyways almost always lead to a kidnapping or mugging, where your characters will have some valuable item stolen. An inn will be able to provide you with shelter, cheese and bread, mutton stew and sour ale. Though the innkeeper will be bad-tempered he may have a pretty daughter who will help travellers escape when the King's soldiers appear in the middle of the night.

Somewhere inside the city will be a temple, palace, castle or great hall. Inside there will be an important item or person that the travellers need to reach. Escape may be necessary and may involve disguises. If a princess is involved she may have to dress up as a stable boy to escape. At this point in the story she may be rather bossy but later on will become more pleasant, because the main character rescues her from a difficult situation caused by her own stubborn behaviour.

The travellers could encounter many different cities. A city of rivers may have many bridges and different types of boats.

Ruined or deserted cities also make good fantasy

locations. These are silent – eerily so. There may be one creature living there such as a cat. Cats may appear to lead travellers into (or out of) danger. Deserted cities may have some remnant of unstable magic left over from a previous time. Do not let anyone ring a bell, bang a gong or eat food that appears at sunset on a table. This is certain to lead to problems. Messages on walls or old tablets of stone may give helpful clues but beware that they are not enchantments that will send you to sleep!

WRITING TIP

You can make sentences more interesting by dropping chunks into them! Here are some ideas:

★ **Use 'who' clauses:**

Stargazer, who was only twelve that year, chased the goats down the hill.

★ **Use 'ing' clauses:**

Stargazer, grabbing the burning flame, darted back into the cave without a moment's thought.

★ **Use 'ed' clauses:**

Stargazer, exhausted from running so far, sat down on a cold rock and waited.

★ **Use descriptive phrases:**

Stargazer, quick and alert, spun round.

★ **Use similes:**

Stargazer, as quick as a cat, pounced!

4. The Mesmerising Mountain Journey

On the quest it is likely that the mountain pass will be blocked. Enemies will be hiding in the mountains. Don't enter caves as this is where trolls and goblins hide out! Also, caves may have disused mineshafts to fall down. So beware!

Unpleasant creatures may live in mountain caves. Dragons will hoard their secret treasure deep inside a mountain. There may be other more unusual and thoroughly nasty creatures in mountain areas, such as orcs, giants and flesh-eating birds.

It was dark inside the cave and it smelled musty. Gardi took off his pack and began to light a fire, using the few pieces of wood they had brought with them. The heat was a welcome relief to the howling storm outside. Silva wondered where the others were and regretted their decision to take the low road. Crest had warned them and he had been right.

As the flames caught, Silva looked round the cave. Someone – or something – had carved drawings onto the walls. They showed animals being slaughtered and villages burned. She shivered and it was not from the cold!

At the back of the cave, high in the ceiling was a hole. And peering through the hole was an eye...

Mountain journeys are nearly always difficult because storms so often prevent travellers from crossing. Darkness descends and the snow is so thick that travellers lose their way. Sometimes one member gets separated from the group and is captured. Occasionally, a frightening creature that turns out to be kind will save them.

The pass over the mountain is narrow and only known to a few chosen people. A great landslide or rocks that have been thrown down by a giant often block it. It may take considerable magic to unblock the route.

Mountain paths wind on, seemingly forever. Packhorses may struggle and donkeys become stubborn with fear. Travellers may have to sleep overnight on a narrow ledge with the storm howling around them. Sleep on a mountain is dangerous, as goblins, dwarves, orcs or ice creatures appear to trap passersby. It is a good idea to save the mountain journey for somewhere near the end of the story as this can make a very exciting scene.

ENCHANTED ENDINGS

Fantasy stories almost always end happily. The bad characters are usually defeated or banished, and the main character may have changed for the better. Stubborn but beautiful princesses will be kinder and spoilt princes have learned to be less selfish. All will have proved themselves to be brave and may have risked their own lives to save others.

It is a good idea to take the main character back to where they began. Endings often involve a simple homecoming back to humble origins – the village or the cottage where the tale started. If the treasure has been lost someone may have managed to tuck away at least one smallish diamond; enough to buy a patch of land and start up an honest trade as a cobbler or bee-keeper.

Here are some possible endings you might consider for your story:

☆ Happily ever after

Everything has been sorted out, all is well and everyone is happy with how the quest has turned out.

☆ Home sweet home

The travellers return to their homes and carry on their daily lives.

☆ All's well (almost)

In this ending everything has turned out well but for one thing that has been lost, left behind or a companion who never made it.

☆ New beginning

Many fantasy stories end by hinting at a new beginning. For example, another quest may just be round the corner!

☆ How they've changed

Make sure that at the end you remind the reader how the main character has changed or what they have learned from their adventures.

TIME TO WRITE

Now it's time to write your story!

1. Go back to the story map in your writing journal and refresh your mind about the plot. When you are writing, use the story map to help shape each scene or chapter. Remember the following things:

★ Write a fantastic opening few lines so that the reader will want to read on;

★ Introduce the task early on;

★ Introduce the 'helper' and think about where their help might be needed;

★ Build each chapter around a setting where something awful happens;

★ Try using the 'rule of three' to build up the excitement;

★ Choose your words carefully, especially the verbs, to add punch to the writing;

★ Vary your sentences and use some 'special effects' like metaphors amd similes.

2. If you get stuck, don't worry — this happens to all writers! You could try:

★ day–dreaming what might happen next;

★ introducing a new and unexpected event;

★ leaving your story for a while and returning to it a few days later.

Now — start writing! Good luck!

EDITING AND PUBLISHING

POLISHING YOUR TALE

So you've finished your story – well done!
What next?

Well before you can say that your fantasy is
finished, you need to check it over. Look for
two things. First, can the writing be improved?
Second, is the writing accurate?

EDITING YOUR STORY

It can help to put your story aside for a few weeks. When
you get it out again, try to re-read it as though you have
never seen it before. This will help you to spot the places
where some rewriting might improve the story. Is
your story gripping? Does it make you want
to read on? Ask a friend to read through
it for you and give you their opinion. All
stories that you buy from bookshops
have been checked like this by an
editor. An editor reads an author's
work, suggests possible improvements

and corrects any inaccuracies before it is published as a book. Here are some things that you (or a friend) might look out for:

1. Possible improvements

☆ Is the quest clear at the beginning?
☆ Have you created a fantastical setting?
☆ Is the main character likeable?
☆ Is the action exciting?
☆ Have you created extraordinary creatures, animals, plants, or places?

☆ Have you avoided streams of speech?
☆ Have you used weak words or clumsy sentences?
☆ Do the sentences in some paragraphs need varying?
☆ Is the ending rushed?

2. Checking for accuracy

☆ Make sure that your spelling, punctuation and paragraphing are all correct.

WRITING TIP

Some authors like to check their work as they write. Others leave the editing until they have finished the whole story. It doesn't matter when you decide to edit – as long as you do it! Make sure you check your work, make improvements and correct any inaccuracies before you move on to the next stage – publishing!

Spelling checklist

If you cannot remember a spelling, you can:

☆ Say the word slowly, listen to each sound and write them down.

☆ Write the word down, look at it and adjust the spelling until the word looks right.

☆ Think of a word you can spell that rhymes with the word you want. The spelling might be similar.

☆ Work out if there are any suffixes, prefixes or a root word that you can spell.

☆ Break the word into syllables and tackle each part at a time.

☆ Use a dictionary or spell check.

Don't avoid using a word because you cannot spell it. Try your best, and when you find out what the correct spelling is, make a note of it in your writing journal to remember for next time.

Punctuation checklist

☆ Make sure that each sentence makes sense and uses a verb (unless it is a one word sentence, such as 'OK?')

☆ Don't forget to use exclamation marks after exclamations, such as 'Go on!'

✫ Remember to use question marks after questions, such as *Where did it go?*

✫ Don't forget commas to separate the things in a list – apart from the final 'and'. For example, *She saw green spiders, purple beetles, pink flies and yellow ants.*

✫ Use a comma to separate an adverb start, such as:
Carefully, she picked up the crystal.

✫ Use a comma to separate 'ing' and 'ed' starts, such as *Screaming in pain, Zennor made her way through the forest.*

✫ Use a comma to separate a subordinate clause at the start of a sentence, such as *While the dwarves ate their meal, Zennor took out the map.*

✫ Use a comma when you drop a phrase or clause into a sentence, such as: *Zennor, tired of the journey, sat down heavily.*

✫ Use speech marks to surround what is spoken (including any punctuation marks in the speech). Use a comma to lead into what is said. When a new speaker says something, start on a new line. For example:
'Pass the salt,' muttered the dragon.
Sal replied, *'here you go.'*

Paragraph checklist

Long paragraphs can be hard to read.
Don't put your readers off!

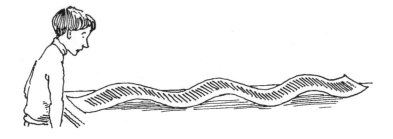

Start a new paragraph with:-
☆ A change of time, for example:
  Early the next morning....
☆ A change of place, for example:
  On the other side of the mountain stood...
☆ A change of action, for example:
  At that moment the lights went out...
☆ A change of character, for example:
  Suddenly, a troll lumbered into view...

PUBLISHING YOUR STORY

After all the time and effort
you have put into writing
your story, you now want
some readers. You can
publish your story in lots
of different ways:
☆ read it aloud;

☆ email it to friends;
☆ turn it into a booklet to give to people;
☆ make a tape recording of it;
☆ upload it on a website.

USEFUL ADDRESSES

☆ Young Writer

This is the national magazine for young writers – and it's brilliant! It has lots of ideas and tips about writing, in-depth interviews with well-known writers and competitions to enter. It also publishes young writers' stories and poems. You can visit the magazine's website at www.youngwriter.org or phone 01544 318901.

☆ www.stonesoup.com

This website belongs to another magazine for young writers. It provides links to loads of other great sites. These will put you in touch with other young writers and give you top writing tips and opportunities to publish your writing on the web.

WRITING TIP

Don't forget to give your story a really gripping title. Most writers leave this until the end as they find that a title often comes to them as they write. Find the right title – and you're finished! Now make sure you publish the results of your hard work!

GLOSSARY

adverb A word that adds meaning to a verb, eg *The goblin ran quickly*.

alliteration A sound effect caused when a sound is repeated in words close together, eg *They ran round the rugged rocks*.

clause A group of words built around a verb, eg *She was thirsty, but she didn't drink*.

comma A punctuation mark (,) used to separate parts of a sentence or items in a list.

complex sentence A sentence with a main clause and one or more subordinate clauses, eg *Tom was ill because he ate too much*.

compound sentence A sentence made up of main clauses joined by a conjunction, eg *I like coffee and I like tea*.

conjunction A word that links clauses or phrases within sentences, eg *Tom was silent and Jerry knew it was the end!*

connective A word or phrase used to link events, eg *The next morning the diamond robbers woke early*.

dialogue The words that characters speak.

dramatic events Exciting events that add tension.

exclamation A sudden expression of emotion using an exclamation mark, eg *'No!'*

fantasy A story containing impossible elements, eg talking trees or singing rocks.

legend A traditional tale, based on truth but embellished over time.

metaphor The technique of writing about something as if it were something else, eg *...the yawning mouth of the cave...*

myth A traditional tale that explains a natural or historical event.

new-universe A story set in an invented new world.

onomatopoeia Words which sound like their meaning, eg *hiss, cuckoo, buzz, crack*.

paragraph A group of sentences that make up a section of writing. New paragraphs begin at a change of time, place, speaker or focus.

personification A technique in which objects are given human characteristics, eg *The wind moaned as if in agony*.

phrase A group of words that work as one unit, eg *the grey-haired, old lady*.

powerful verbs Verbs that show action and are expressive, eg using *dashed, scuttled* or *darted* to describe how a character moves.

quest A journey to find something or someone.

'sentence of three' A type of sentence structure that is useful for description and pace, eg *Stargazer wore a pointy hat, a sky-red coat and a pair of baggy trousers*.

settings Where a story takes place.

simile A technique in which the writer compares one thing to another, eg *The moon was like a thin smile* or *The moon was as thin as a fingernail*.

simple sentence A sentence of one clause, eg *The little elf went to bed*.

speech marks Also called punctuation marks ('') these are used to enclose spoken words eg, *'I can't remember meeting a kinder fairy,'* smiled Venka.

subordinate clause A clause that relies on a main clause for its meaning, eg *The bird flew <u>because it had wings</u>*.

thesaurus A type of dictionary that provides alternatives to words, eg *eat – scoff, chew, munch, gobble*, etc.

verb A 'being' or 'doing' word, eg *She <u>crawled</u> down the lane. She <u>felt</u> petrified*.

INDEX